James Halliwell-Phillipps

New lamps or old?

A few additional words on the momentous question

James Halliwell-Phillipps

New lamps or old?
A few additional words on the momentous question

ISBN/EAN: 9783337303532

Printed in Europe, USA, Canada, Australia, Japan

Cover: Foto ©Andreas Hilbeck / pixelio.de

More available books at **www.hansebooks.com**

New Lamps or Old?

A FEW ADDITIONAL WORDS

ON

THE MOMENTOUS QUESTION

Respecting the E and the A

IN THE NAME OF

Our National Dramatist.

SECOND EDITION.

It is said that his surname was Quixada or Quesada, for, in this particular, the authors who have mentioned the subject do not agree. There are, however, very probable reasons for conjecturing that he was called Quixana. But this is of little importance to our story. Let it suffice that, in narrating, we do not swerve a jot from the truth.—*The Life and Adventures of Don Quixote de la Mancha.*

BRIGHTON :

PRINTED BY MESSRS. FLEET AND BISHOP.

1880.

NOTE.

The subject of our early nominal orthography, discussed in the following pages, has elicited so wide an interest, apart from the individual question, that I have been induced to reprint the pamphlet with a few additions and corrections.

The special case which has occasioned this investigation may thus be briefly epitomized. There having been no standard for the spelling of names in the time of Shakespeare, it follows, of course, that one form of signature was then as correct, or as incorrect, as another, that it was no authority for a printed orthography, and that the election of an uniform mode can be left to modern usage. In selecting, in the case of Shakespeare, the longest form, we are guided by the probability, almost the certainty, founded on the dedications to the first poems, that the great dramatist himself, had he lived to have superintended the publication of an edition of his works, would have adopted in that edition the orthography of his name which was sanctioned by his intimate friends and colleagues when they edited the folio of 1623, the complete form, Shakespeare, accepted with a singular unanimity by Ben Jonson and other contemporaries.

J. O. HALLIWELL-PHILLIPPS.

Hollingbury Copse,
    Brighton,
        3rd April, 1880.

A FEW WORDS, &c.

A FEW weeks ago, under the impression that it would be as well, if it were possible, that there should be uniformity in the printed orthography of the name of our national dramatist, I ventured to issue a little tentative pamphlet on the subject. The question was obviously an excessively trivial one in itself, and the idea of its discussion, had it referred to any but the greatest of England's sons, would have been positively ludicrous. No one would have imagined that such an enquiry could have raised the smallest of storms in the minutest of teapots. Nevertheless, the few pages alluded to created in their way quite a little hubbub. Besides an excellent leading article in one of the prominent London dailies, there were a score of other notices showing the interest a resuscitation of an old difficulty had excited. One writer, indeed, in a letter in the Daily News of December the 20th, was positively stimulated to compare the reluctance to adopt the shorter form of the poet's name with the fearful obstruction of " Toryism " to everything that is correct and proper. From the expressions used by the individual in question it may be inferred that, in his opinion, the Tories, having done their best to prevent the introduction of Free Trade and the Reform Bill, are now completing their iniquities by spelling the name of the great dramatist in the way in which he himself printed it in the first editions of his own poems; that the vagabonds who write *Shakespeare* are bucolic and pig-headed Conservatives, and that the angels who prefer *Shakspere* are advanced and enlightened Radicals. As if to crown this edifice of bluster, in another journal I was personally battered merely because I had had the audacity to advocate the retention of the *e* and the *a*. When Bedreddin Hassan was told that his life was to be forfeited for omitting to add pepper to the cream-tart, he could hardly have been more astonished than myself at this funny display of gratuitous irritability.

In contrast to those who take such a vital interest in the suppression of the *e* and the *a* that they allow their little feelings to run away with them in the face of opposition, there are others who ridicule the idea of the matter being worth discussion at all. The latter view is well put in the Echo of December the 4th in allusion to my pamphlet,—" he adopts Shakespeare, with which nobody can quarrel ;—indeed, nobody would quarrel with him if he spelt the name backwards ;—it is of more importance to read Shakespeare's works, and, above all, to understand and profit by them, than to give reasons for putting in or leaving out an x in his name." Certainly, for ourselves and to ourselves the immortal text is all-sufficient, and the elucidation of that text is the only really good use of Shakespearean criticism, but surely there is a respect due to the memory of the greatest name in our literature. It is not courteous to that memory to speak as if it were of no sort of consequence whether we alluded to the great poet as William Shakespeare or as Tony Lumpkin. With due deference, therefore, to the opinion of our reverberating contemporary, I shall endeavour to follow the lead of my adverse critics in treating the subject as one of the most serious and weighty enquiries of the present day, as, in short, the great problem of all, the momentous question whether we are to discard or retain the e and the a in the spelling of the name of our national dramatist. My chief fear is that the enquiry into this important mystery may not be approached with the complete solemnity due to an investigation of such paramount gravity ; but it shall at all events be treated fairly and dispassionately.

Previously to opening a discussion of this kind it may be well to observe that, in treating a subject which involves a consideration of the usages of a remote age, it is essentially necessary to eliminate from our minds any influence exercised by the knowledge of those of our own. This is especially necessary in the present instance. In these days a person's signature is, in nine hundred and ninety-nine cases out of a thousand, absolute evidence of the acknowledged orthography of his own name and of that of his family. In Shakespeare's time, a person's signature, in a corresponding number of cases, was no evidence at all of the correct orthography of his own name or of that of his relatives.

The truth of this latter position can be demonstrated by hundreds of illustrations. Colonel Chester, one of the best living authorities in such matters, after mentioning the numerous instances he had met with of capricious forms of early signatures of the same name in the University books at Oxford, writes, —" my experience among other records has been the same, and I should as soon doubt the existence of Hollingbury Copse as the position

you assume, that there was no settled orthography of surnames in the time of Shakespeare." But although the fact is acknowledged
by all who have carefully examined the subject,
a few examples should be given for the sake of
the many who have had no opportunity of
doing so. Thus, Lord Robert Dudley's signature was Dudley or Duddeley, and his wife's,
Duddley. Allen, the actor, signed his name at
various times, Alleyn, Aleyn, Allin, and Allen,
while his wife's signature appears as Alleyne.
Henslowe's autographs are in the forms of
Hensley, Henslow, and Henslowe. Samuel
Rowley signed himself Rouley, Rowley, and
Rowleye. Burbage sometimes wrote Burbadg
while his brother signed himself Burbadge.
One of the poet's sons-in-law wrote himself
Quyney, Quyneye, and Conoy, while his brother,
the curate, signed, Quiney. His other son-in-
law, Dr. Hall, signed himself Hawle and Hall.
Alderman Sturley, of Stratford-on-Avon, signed
his name sometimes in that form and sometimes, Strelly, both forms being used in letters
written to the same person in the same year,
1598. Sir Walter Raleigh signed both Rauley
and Ralegh, and Sir Philip Sidney both Sydney
and Sidney. An actor contemporary with Shakespeare wrote himself Downton, Dowten, and

Dowton. The signature of a sixteenth century earl was Shrewsbury, that of his wife Shrowesbury. Different members of the Trevelyan family sign themselves, Trevelyan, Trevilian, Trevillian, Trevylyan, Trevelian, Trevylian. Richard Hathaway sometimes so wrote his name and sometimes Hathway. Thomas Nash, who married the poet's grand-daughter, signed himself both Nash and Nashe. Simon Trap, curate of Stratford-upon-Avon, wrote his name Trapp and Trappe. In a manuscript pedigree of 1613 at the Heralds' College a gentleman signs his name Payne, his nephew's signature on the same day in the same manuscript being Pain. Shakespeare's parents could not write at all, and the only signatures of any of their children known to exist are those of the poet, and that of his brother Gilbert, the latter signing his name Shakespere, that is, with the important central e. These instances will suffice for the demonstration of the main position, that in former days there was no established nominal orthography. As Sam Weller observed, "it all depended upon the taste and fancy of the speller, my Lord," and it would be difficult to state the usage of Shakespeare's time in more forcible language. It is curious that there are still to be found lingering traces of the old uncertainty. My old friend, Mr. Joseph Clarke, F.S.A., of the Roos, Co. Essex, tells me of a small tradesman in the country whose signature was capriciously either Travers or Travis. Upon his father, an old man, being asked which was the correct form, he replied that "one way was as good as the other." Professor Baynes furnishes me with a still more curious example in that of a Somersetshire gardener who writes his name Nipcote, his brother, Nitcote, while other members of the family use such variations as Nepcot and Netcot.

It is obvious then, even to the typical schoolboy, that it would be unreasonable to attempt to follow individual signatures in the modern orthography of names of the Shakespearean period. If we were to do so, we should write Lord Dudley and Lady Duddley, Lord Shrewsbury and Lady Shrowesbury, Thomas Quyney and the Rev. George Quiney, Mr. Allen and Mrs. Alleyne, Mr. Payne and his nephew Mr. Pain, Alderman Sturley in one month and Alderman Strelly in the next, Dr. Hall at one period of his life and Dr. Hawle at another. When mentioning the great dramatist we should be at liberty to write his name in two or three ways, but not in the form used by his brother Gilbert Shakespere, and in alluding to another great poet we should write Milton, but his second daughter must be introduced as a Millton. Heywood the epigrammatist would become Heywod, Cardinal Wolsey must be Cardinal Wulcy, Lords Leicester and Warwick would appear as Leycester and Warwyke, Herrick would be Hearick, Nichols would be transformed into Nycowlles, and so on to any number of similar inconvenient variations.

It is simply casual ingenuity which suggests the deflection of caprice into ignorance under the accusation that Shakespeare, and those numerous contemporaries who varied their signatures, did not know how to spell their own names. Well, they didn't, for the simple reason that names in those days had not been subjected to any rules of orthography, that the attainment of what we should call orthographical accuracy was at that time impossible, and it is obviously improper to sneer at them for indulging in a fanciful practice then as common with the learned as with the illiterate. One of the most accomplished scholars of the sixteenth century signed himself either Ascham or Askham, and it might of course be said that he did not know how to write his own name, but it would be fairer to observe that there was in those days no established orthography, no method of spelling sanctioned by usage or authority either in surnames or Christian names, or in the English language generally. We have already seen that there was none in surnames, and as to Christian names the varieties are equally perplexing. Shakespeare's friend and neighbour, Mr. Shawe, spelt his in the following very extraordinary number of ways, — Julyus, Julius, Julie, Julyne, Jule, Julines, Julynes, July, Julye, Julyius and Julyles. As for orthography in language either in books or manuscripts of the Shakespearean period, all who are familiar with such matters know that the same word is frequently spelt in half-a-dozen various forms in a single page.

The choice of the pronunciation of Shakespeare's name is of course a question independent of the form in which it should be printed. The general instinct seems to be adverse to the ancient orthoepy of Shaxpere, and the main reason against the prudence of adopting the short form is that it might encourage the name to be so spoken. There can be little doubt that the poet was generally called Shaxpere or Shaxper in the provinces, but certainly not always. In the earliest known document respecting any member of the poet's family, one which refers to property at Snitterfield near

Stratford-on-Avon, the name of his grandfather is given as Shakespere, showing the first syllable to be long, and in the local manuscripts in which his father is continually mentioned, the name of the latter is variously written, Shakspeyr, Shaxspere, Shacksper, Shaksperc, Shakyspere, Shakespere, Shaxpeare, Shakspeir, Shakysper, Shaxpere, Shakspearc, Shackespere, Schackspere, Shakspeyre, Shaksper, and Shakespeare, without the slightest notion of uniformity. The transcriber of the parish register is the most consistent, the majority of entries in that record being Shakspere, but even there we have also the forms of Shakspeer, Shaxspere, and Shakspeare. The poet's intimate friends had clearly no notion that they were to spell his name in any particular fashion. Richard Quiney in 1598 addressed his celebrated letter " to my loveinge good frend and countreyman Mr. Wm. Shackespere." Alderman Sturley speaks of him in the same year as Mr. Shaksper. The great dramatist's kinsman and solicitor, Thomas Greene, wrote his client's name Shakspear, Shakspeare, and Shakspurre, and Mrs. and Mr. Hall, the poet's daughter and son-in-law, who must have known the correct orthography, had there been any settled form at the time, spell the name Shakspeare in the monumental inscription to him while it is Shakespeare in that to his wife. Can anything more clearly show that nominal spelling was in those days a simple matter of chance or fancy?

There were occasional and rare exceptions, the most notable and illustrative being that of "rare Ben," who, although he apparently did not take the trouble to remonstrate with those friends who wrote and printed his name Johnson, appears, judging from the dozens of his signatures in existence, to have invariably written Jonson. This was probably to distinguish it from the commoner name, and, to the best of my belief, although I have not had the opportunity of verifying the fact, the shorter form is used in all his own printed dedicatory epistles. If Shakespeare's case were at all similar, if we had possessed numerous examples of his uniform signature* at various periods of life, and if the name in his dedications had appeared in the same form, then there would have been of course an end of the matter. But the facts do not bear out an important similarity. In those deeply interesting epistles to Lord Southampton, the

---

* But this in itself would go for very little. A celebrated earl invariably signed himself Leycester, yet no writer, treating of the Elizabethan period, would consider it necessary to introduce that antiquated orthography.

only letters of the great dramatist known to exist, attached to the only works we can confidently believe to have been issued with his sanction, the name appears in its full proportions with both the *e* and the *a*. These dedications, to Venus and Adonis in 1593 and to Lucrece in 1594, are to my mind absolutely conclusive of the general question.

There is no good pretence for raising a doubt of the generally acknowledged fact that those poems were issued under Shakespeare's immediate authority. The personal character of the dedications might alone suffice to indicate that this was the case. Not only was there no theatrical management to interfere with the copyright, as was the case with respect to most if not all of his plays, and no symptoms of the bookselling special interest in either of the publications, but both of them were printed, as Mr. Payne Collier* was the first to point out, by a

---

* This mention of my old friend's name gives me the opportunity of observing that, although, as it has been recently stated, I was the founder of the old Shakespeare Society, yet it was entirely owing to Mr. Collier's influence and active co-operation that the Society was ever established. Under his judicious and genial management every variety of Shakespearean opinion received friendly attention, the Society, during the thirteen years (1841 to 1853) of its existence, doing good and useful work quietly and amicably. Alas that it was not resuscitated on its

native of Stratford-on-Avon and the son of one of John Shakespeare's intimate friends. Every circumstance, indeed, connected with the publication of Venus and Adonis and Lucrece tends to show that they were printed under the author's sanction.

Under any circumstances, it is evident that Shakespeare had a voice in the matter with the printer or publisher when he proceeded to dedicate a second work to the same nobleman. Can any one believe that, if the great dramatist had really cared to have his name spelt without the *e* and the *a*, he would have permitted the longer form to remain in the second dedication ? Is it not clear that, whatever phases his signature may have assumed, he either wished, or, at the very least, tacitly admitted that he did not dislike his name appearing as Shakespeare in his own printed works ? Another piece of corroborative evidence is at the end of a poem which he contributed to Chester's Loves Martyr, 1601, and which could hardly have been inserted without his direct sanction. As if to place the matter beyond all doubt, his name is there

original basis of common-sense criticism when my late dear friend, Howard Staunton, so ardently desired and had practically commenced its revival in 1872 ! Let me here gratefully add how much I personally owed in early life to Mr. Collier's kind and unselfish encouragement.

printed with both the disputed letters and with a hyphen. See the annexed facsimile of the conclusion of this poem. The printed literature of Shakespeare's time is all but unanimous in the adoption of the longer orthography, and in it there are very few instances indeed of the omission of either the *e* or the *a*, while there are numerous examples of the occurrence of the full name with a hyphen, as in the poem just mentioned and in the Sonnets, published in 1609, where the hyphened name is given at length upwards of thirty times. It is, in fact, exceedingly curious that one form of a name of such easy variation should have been so generally adopted in print at a time when there was great laxity in such matters in printed books as well as in writings. Thus, in the interesting collection, England's Parnassus, 1600, while the name of one poet is spelt in four different ways,—Achilley, Achelly, Achellye, Achely,—and rare Ben's appears both as Johnson and Jhonson, that of the great dramatist is uniformly printed Shakespeare in upwards of forty instances in that small volume. I will now proceed to a consideration of the poet's five acknowledged signatures, the only examples of undoubted authenticity known to exist.

1. Indenture of Bargain to Shakespeare

Threnos.

BEautie, Truth, and Raritie,
Grace in all ſimplicitie,
Here encloſde, in cinders lie.

Death is now the *Phœnix* neſt,
And the *Turtles* loyall breſt,
To eternitie doth reſt.

Leauing no poſteritie,
Twas not their infirmitie,
It was married Chaſtitie.

Truth may ſeeme, but cannot be,
Beautie bragge, but tis not ſhe,
Truth and Beautie buried be.

To this vrne let thoſe repaire,
That are either true or faire,
For theſe dead Birds, ſigh a prayer.

William Shake-ſpeare.

of a house in Blackfriars, 10 March, 1613,* the original deed being now in the Guildhall Library. Here the signature is unquestionably Shakspere, reading the contraction as *er*, and considering that which follows the *e* as a mere flourish. Sir F. Madden, indeed, reads the last syllable *per* and thinks that the contraction is for the final *e*. The same result follows from either theory, but the latter one would, I fancy, be more likely to be correct if it had referred to a document of an earlier date. The former is confirmed by what is apparently a very careful facsimile made by the elder Ireland soon after the discovery of the indenture, his original tracing being now in my possession.

2. Mortgage Deed of the same house, dated 11 March, 1613, now in the British Museum. Here again we have a contracted form, the only written letters of the second syllable being *spe*, but the mark of contraction is different from that in the previous deed, it appearing in this one as if it were an *a* in the published facsimile

---

* The original indenture of conveyance to Shakespeare, dated on the same day, is in my possession, and one of my choicest treasures. This deed, that which was enrolled in Chancery, is in fine and perfect condition, with the original official note of enrollment on the outside. It is endorsed,--*Walker et Shakespeare et al.*

of 1790, and *u* in recent copies, in either case implying, to judge from the usual meaning of abbreviations of the time, that an *a* was one of the letters of what was intended. The contraction is also clearly given as an *a* in Malone's original tracing made in the year 1784, and although he afterwards thought " that what was supposed to be that letter was only a mark of abbreviation with a turn or curl at the first part of it, which gave it the appearance of a letter," this latter notion was a mere conjecture hazarded without the advantage of another reference to the original (Inquiry, 1796, pp. 118-120), and is an opinion which will not stand the test of a close examination. Many years ago, the original deed now in the Museum was kindly brought to my house by its then owner, Mr. Troward, and my late valued friend, Mr. Fairholt, took the greatest pains on that occasion to make an accurate tracing of the poet's signature. The engraving from that facsimile may be seen in my folio edition of Shakespeare, vol. i., p. 209, and there the contraction is more like *a* than *u*, encouraging a suspicion that the top part of the former letter has been obliterated by the handling of the deed during the long period that has elapsed since the autograph was first traced by Malone.

Whether there is a probability in this suggestion might perhaps be decided by the use of a microscope; but, at all events, the form of Shakspere cannot in this instance be admitted with anything like certainty.

The exact interpretation of this second autograph is, however, of little moment in our enquiry, for, as it has been well observed, "the contractions exhibited by these two signatures neutralize their evidence," and Shakespeare clearly intended by using those contractions that his name should be included within the narrow limits of the seal-labels. There are then, as absolute evidences of the poet's usage in his signatures, merely the three appended to the will, and these must ·be examined in· detail,—

1. The first is now extremely indistinct, having suffered from the wear and tear of the manuscript. That it was originally Shakspere may be safely concluded from the facsimile made by Steevens in 1776. Dr. Farmer also personally examined the document when it was in a more perfect state, and he confirms this reading in a manuscript note of his in my possession.

2. There is more doubt about the second one, the space between the p and the r apparently

indicating the original presence of two letters, which were read *ea* by Dr. Farmer, but, judging from the best facsimiles, and without a new inspection of the original, it is my conviction that here we should read Shakspere, the minute blank between the *e* and the *r* being occasioned by the intervention of the loop of a letter hanging from the body of the will. Here again the microscope might be of use.

3. In the last autograph the second syllable appears to be *speare* in all the facsimiles, as it does in that of Steevens made in the year 1776, and then so accepted by Malone. The latter writer, indeed, afterwards changed his opinion, not, however, from a second examination of the original, but merely because an anonymous correspondent was of opinion that "though there was a superfluous stroke when the poet came to write the letter *r* in his last signature, probably from the tremor of his hand, there was no *a* discoverable in that syllable," Inquiry, 1796, p. 118. The notion of the tremor of the hand is simply gratuitous, the will having been executed more than a month before the death of the poet, and there being no evidence that he was then invalided. Be this as it may, the correspondent's surmise cannot invalidate the authority of Steevens's own tracing in

the original of which, still preserved, the letter *a* is clearly exhibited, the accuracy of the facsimile being ratified by the following note, — *G. Steevens delineavit accurante et testante Edmondo Malone,* 1776. That there are two letters between the *p* and the *r* seems beyond a reasonable doubt, and a writer in the Gentleman's Magazine for June, 1789, reads *speere,* but surely the formation of the writing supports our first interpretation. But what about the first syllable of the auto-graph ? A distinguished scholar has just pointed out to me—and it is, as in the case of the management of the egg by Columbus, most singularly curious so obvious a fact should have escaped the notice of all others—that the character following the letter *k* is the then well-known and accepted contraction* for *es*. There cannot be a doubt on this point, and therefore the poet's last signature appears in his own selected literary form of Shakespeare.

Malone expatiates on the "very extraordinary circumstance that a man should write his name twice one way, and once another, on the same

---

* Mr. Hardy, Appendix to Fortieth Report on the Public Records, p. 567, observes that this contraction "*generally* occurs at the end of words." Its situation in this signature is peculiar and difficult of explanation.

paper," Inquiry, p. 117; but it is not certain that the three signatures were written on the same day. At that period, the two first would not necessarily require the attendance of witnesses, and might have been added when the will was first copied ready for signing in January, or at any time between then and Lady Day.* On a careful examination it will be seen that the last signature differs somewhat in formation from the others, especially in that of the capital letter W. But even supposing that all the signatures were attached to the will on the same day, a variation in their forms would not be more extraordinary than that of Walter Roche, the poet's schoolmaster, signing his name twice in different ways on the same day in the same document, or than Margaret Trevelyan at a later period writing her own name and that of her husband with different spellings in the very same line,—" Margaret Trevelyan, for her husband George Trevelian." Sir William Brown, who signed indiscriminately in at least three different ways, spells his name Browne in a letter to Lord Sidney, May 24th, 1604, and Broune in another

---

* There was so much laxity in such matters excepting in the presence of witnesses at the final signature, it is not at all unlikely that the day of the later month is incorrect. At all events it is singular that the will should be executed on the very same day of March on which it was originally dated in January.

letter written on the very next day to the same
nobleman. I possess an indenture of the year
1692, in which one party signs his name
Banckyes, his uncle Banckys, and his mother
Bancks, all written on the same day. A
little more research would no doubt produce
many other like examples, although the extraordinary laxity formerly displayed by nearly
every one in the orthography of surnames
scarcely requires more confirmatory evidence.
This is, in fact, the whole gist of the matter,
that the forms of autographs were in those
days no reliable guides for an uniform printed
usage, and, as I ventured to say in my
other pamphlet, " to follow signatures would
revolutionize the whole system of early nominal
orthography, and lead to preposterous results."

Now, in conclusion, with a flourish of mag-
nanimity. If it be possible that any earnest
Shakespearean student, after perusing the above
luminous exposition, can wish to discard the
e and the *a*, he has my solemn assurance
that I shall not have the slightest inclination
either to roar him down or quarrel with him
on that account. On the contrary, if such
an individual appear and will favour me with
a visit, he shall be received with all the attention due to a rara avis at my primitive and

ornithological bungalow. Although my library is small, it includes some of the choicest Shakespearean rarities in the world, and there is also an unrivalled collection of drawings and engravings illustrative of the life of the great dramatist. A mere glance over the latter will occupy a summer's day. And the feast of reason shall be irrigated by the flow of port, claret, or madeira, and by what is not now to be seen every day of the week, really old sherry. If, unfortunately, he has forsworn racy potations and not discovered that good sherris-sack "ascends into the brain and dries there all the foolish, and dull, and crudy vapours which environ it," then are there our deep chalk wells, yielding an inexhaustible supply of the pure aqueous element as bright and sparkling as the waves and atmosphere of Brighton herself.

J. O. HALLIWELL-PHILLIPPS.

Hollingbury Copse,
    Brighton,
        January, 1880.

NOTICES OF THE PRESS.

How shall we spell the name of Shakspere? A pamphlet, bearing the signature of a Shaksperian expert, and the title, New Lamps or Old, revives this debated point in "A Few Additional Words on the Momentous Question Respecting the E and the A in the Name of Our National Dramatist." The writer, as is well known, defends Shakespeare against all other forms, and in spite of the signatures of Shakspere himself. His contention is that in Shakspere's time there was really no settled orthography, and that names were frequently signed differently on the same day and by the same person. Shakspere, contends Mr. Halliwell-Phillipps, did exactly what was done by his contemporaries. He used contractions and spelled his name according to the whim or desire of the moment. But in the works published under his supervision he adopted the full form Shakespeare. The deeply interesting epistles to Lord Southampton have the signature with the *e* and the *a*, and are " absolutely conclusive on the general question." It is evident that the contempories of Shakspere were as lax as Shakspere himself is alleged to have been in the spelling of the name. Richard Quiney wrote Shakespere, Alderman Sturley wrote Shaksper, Thomas Greene spelled the name in three different ways, while in Stratford Church the name on the monument is Shakspeare while on the monument of the poet's wife it is Shakespeare. After reading all this and a great deal more very interesting evidence in favour of Shakespeare, those who have adopted Shakspere will adhere to that form for the best of all reasons— they have it in the poet's own handwriting in the majority of his accepted signatures. Mr. Halliwell-Phillipps maintains that it would be preposterous to follow signatures when we have access to a selected literary form. But this seems very like saying that we must refuse evidence which brings us directly into contact

with Shakspere personally, and rely on a form which may or
may not have had his deliberate sanction. When we look on
the signatures we see evidence supplied by Shakspere himself ;
when we look at the dedications of Venus and Adonis we see
evidence supplied by a printer.* No wonder then that some
of us, with all deference to a most conscientious, diligent, and
able scholar, prefer Shakspere.—*Western Daily Press.*

Mr. J. O. Halliwell-Phillipps has materially strengthened his
argument in favour of spelling the name of our greatest poet
with the additional *e* after *k*,—Shakespeare, in "A Few Additional Words on the Momentous Question respecting the E and
the A in the name of our National Dramatist." We quite agree
with him that there ought to be uniformity in this matter. It
is surely time we arrived at a determination concerning it.
Our own argument has been that while we receive the name as
Shake-speare in pronunciation, the poet has not used the *e* after
the *k* in any of his signatures remaining to us. The suggestion
now is that in one of the signatures to the will the character
following the letter *k* is the then well-known and accepted contraction for *es*. This, if established, should suffice to settle the
matter. The objection that will probably be taken is the in-
frequency of the use of that contraction anywhere but at the
end of a word. If, however, we remember that in some of the
dedications the word is divided by a hyphen, its introduction
before the hyphen might be accepted as probable.—*The Builder.*

To the antiquary there are no such things as trifles ; to the
Englishman everything connected with the name of Shakspere
is sacred. Hence it can excite no surprise to find that a viva-
cious controversy is now proceeding as to the proper spelling of
Shakspere's name. There has always been a curious want of
uniformity in the orthographical presentation of the surname of
our national dramatist. Dr. Johnson, Rowe, and other com-

---

* This is adroitly but not very fairly put. The balance of
probability is clearly in favour of the printed form having been
sanctioned by the poet himself.—J. O. H.-P.

mentators spell it Shakspeare ; Dyce and Cowden Clarke say Shakespeare; in the folio of his works, brought out by his own intimate associates, the form of Shakespeare is used. The Stratford register contains entries of the poet's baptism and death, of the baptism of his children, and the death of his son. In these the name is uniformly spelled Shakspere. The quarto editions of the plays, and, what is still more important, the editions of the poems issued during his lifetime say Shake-speare. Of manuscript evidence there is, unfortunately, very little, and it is not quite consistent. There are only five signatures of the poet that are beyond all doubt authentic. The signatures to the indenture of bargain and mortgage deed of the house in Blackfriars are both contracted so as to get the name included within the narrow limits of the seal label, and it has been said that the varying " contractions exhibited by these two signatures neutralise their evidence." So far as they go, one appears to be Shakspere, but the other is more doubtful. There remain, then, the three signatures to the will. The first is admittedly Shakspere ; the space between the *e* and the *r* of the second signature was read *ea* by Dr. Farmer, but Mr. Halliwell-Phillipps is of opinion that the minute blank was caused by the intervention of the loop of a letter hanging from the body of the will. The third signature was given in all the fac-similes as Shakspeare, though Malone afterwards thought there was reason for discarding the *a*. Such, in brief, is the body of evidence. Of late years greater favour has been given to the shorter forms of Shakspere's name, and Mr. J. O. Halli-well - Phillipps on recently advocating the longer form was assailed by an outcry of Toryism. Undaunted by his opponents, Mr. Halliwell-Phillipps returns to the charge, and in a pamphlet bearing the title of Old Lamps and New sets forth his reasons for desiring to retain " the *e* and the *a* in the name of our national dramatist." The first matter to be remembered is that in Shakspere's days there was no settled orthography of sur-names. In local MSS. the name of the poet's family is given as Shakspeyr, Shaxspere, Schacksper, Shakyspere, Shaxpeare, and other forms, without the slightest uniformity. Mr. Halliwell-

Phillipps lays stress upon the fact that the subscriptions to the dedications of the poems is in the longest form of the name. "Is it not clear," he asks, "that, whatever phases his signature may have assumed, he either wished, or at least tacitly admitted, that he did not dislike his name appearing as Shakespeare in his own printed works?" The same form is used at the end of the poem in Chester's Love's Martyr, 1601, whilst the printed literature of the time " is all but unanimous " in using it. On the other hand, there is one argument not to be disdained for the spelling Shakspere. It is the shortest orthography that has yet been proposed, and that in a busy age is a very great recommendation.—*The Manchester Guardian.*

Mr. J. O. Halliwell-Phillipps has just issued an interesting little pamphlet, full of both erudition and humour, on the mode of spelling the name of the national dramatist. He argues that Shakespeare is the proper manner, commencing his observations by amusing references to the virulence of some gentlemen of the "intense" sort, who compared the reluctance to adopt the shorter form of the poet's name with the fearful obstruction of Toryism to everything that is correct and proper. Mr. Halliwell-Phillipps proceeds to point out that in the dramatist's time a person's signature was scarcely evidence at all of the correct orthography of his own name or that of his relatives. He instances a number of examples in which a man signed his name in one way and his wife in another, and of two or three forms of signature by one individual. Thus, says the author, one of the poet's sons-in-law wrote himself Quyney, Quyneye, and Conoy, while his brother, the curate, signed Quiney, His other son-in-law, Dr. Hall, signed himself Hawle and Hall. Thomas Nash, who married the poet's granddaughter, signed himself both Nash and Nashe. In point of fact, people in those days signed their names according to taste or momentary caprice. Mr. Halliwell-Phillipps examines the acknowledged signatures of the poet ; and dismissing those of the indenture of of bargain of the house in Blackfriars and of the mortgage deed of the same property as having contracted letters, and therefore useless for the purposes of the inquiry, he proceeds to consider the three signatures affixed to the will. The first autograph he pronounces to be Shakspere, the second probably the same, while the third he concludes was Shakespeare, which was also the printed signature affixed to the dedications of the poems. The pamphlet comes to a close with a funny but highly genial invitation from the accomplished and kindly old scholar, asking those who disagree with him to pay him a visit at Hollingbury Copse and discuss the matter amicably over some " really old sherry."—*Birmingham Daily Globe.*

Mr. J. O. Halliwell-Phillipps, the well-known Shakspearean scholar and enthusiast, has written a pamphlet some thirty pages long in order to settle for ever the momentous question "respecting the E and the A in the name of our National Dramatist." A very bright and sparkling brochure is this controversial tract dated from Hollingbury Copse, Brighton ; but its most original feature is a hospitable invitation to Shakspearean students—and they must be legion—to visit the author and look over his library, containing " the choicest Shakspearean rarities in the world, and an unrivalled collection of drawings and engravings illustrative of the life of the great dramatist." Nay, more, Mr. Halliwell-Phillipps promises to entertain his guests in splendid fashion. "The feast of reason,' he says, " shall be irrigated by the flow of port, claret, or madeira, and by what is not now to be seen every day of the week, really good sherry." As for the teetotallers, they are promised "an inexhaustible supply of the pure aqueous element from our deep chalk wells." But, supposing all the Shakspearean students in the United Kingdom accepted the universal invitation on the same day, how long would the cellars or the wells of Hollingbury Copse hold out ?—*The Illustrated London News.*

THE LIFE OF SHAKESPEARE.

Under the title of *Contributions towards a Life of Shakespeare*, it is possible, health, strength, and inclination permitting, that I may some day commence a series of folio volumes in which I should hope to fully investigate the truth or probability of every recorded incident in the personal and literary history of the great dramatist, and to include a vast mass of correlative information, the accumulation of many years' researches, the whole to be copiously illustrated with wood engravings and fac-similes. Amongst the latter would be fac-similes of every known contemporary document in which the name of the poet appears.

It is scarcely necessary to observe that the compilation of a satisfactory life of Shakespeare is an impossibility. A biography without correspondence, without details of conversation, and without any full contemporary delineations of character, must necessarily be fragmentary. There is, however, more to be learned respecting the history of the poet's career than many people would imagine, and some new facts and much that is suggestive that have not yet been published. Moreover, a new and most interesting source of information has just unexpectedly opened, and this circumstance has tended more than anything else to overcome my increasing reluctance to encounter the worries of publication. Researches, at least in my case, are not energetically carried on if there is no ultimate view of some use being made of the results. A part of my scheme would include minute details respecting the condition of Stratford-on-Avon in the time of the poet, and generally, as was stated when I projected a similar work in 1874, to give notices of his surroundings, that is to say, amongst others, of the members of his family, the persons with whom he associated, the books he used, the stage on which he acted, the estates he purchased, the houses and towns in which he resided, and the country through which he travelled. The consideration of these and similar topics will not be without its biographical value. It will bring us nearer to a knowledge of Shakespeare's personality if we can form even an approximate idea of the condition of England and its people in his own day, the sort of places in which he lived, how he made his fortune, the occupations and social positions of his relatives and friends, the nature of the ancient stage, and the usages of contemporary domestic life.

The numerous traditions respecting the great dramatist have never been minutely investigated. It is astonishing how long personal traditions lingered in the provinces before the newspaper age, and any that can be traced even so far back as the last century deserve careful examination. There are many that are sheer inventions, others extremely doubtful, but some that can be partially authenticated. In this department of the biography I have had the advantage of a close friendship and numerous discussions on the subject with the late R. B. Wheler and W. O. Hunt, of Stratford-on-Avon, the last links of the traditional period. All genuine oral traditions have now expired, but unfortunately a considerable number of similar stories have been unblushingly fabricated in even recent years. The assurance with which these have been uttered would be amusing were it not so mischievous.

Charles Dickens, in one of his hasty letters, writes thus:—"The life of Shakespeare is a fine mystery, and I tremble every day lest something should come up." Now, if I thought that there were even a remote chance of a revelation that would exhibit Shakespeare in the light of one who could in any fairness be termed a bad man, my inquisitive researches would not be continued. But there is too abundant favourable evidence of his general character to render such a contingency possible. That he was wild in his youth, that he sometimes drank a little more wine than was good for him, and that he occasionally flirted with the young ladies at the Bankside more freely than Mrs. Shakespeare at Stratford-on-Avon would have approved of, may be conceded by those who do not consider it requisite to assume that the greatest of poets must necessarily be the greatest of saints. But that he deliberately would either have ruined the character of another, or betrayed the domestic confidence of a friend or host, is too inconsistent with the contemporary opinions of his character to be at all credible. With the exception of a tale that is a palpable fabrication, the Davenant story is the only recorded one respecting Shakespeare which, if true, would really involve an accusation of criminality; but so difficult is it to eradicate scandal, however baseless, .that the tale has been accepted as truthful for many generations and by even recent writers. It is, therefore, with peculiar satisfaction that, after the lapse of nearly three centuries, I can announce the discovery of contemporary evidences which prove decisively that there is not a word of truth in the libel.

The first volume of the projected series could not be completed at the earliest before the Spring of next year.

I do not intend to receive subscribers' names, as the work will not be so published. If it ever appear, it will be obtainable only through a special London agent, and the impression will be extremely limited. This preliminary announcement is made in the hope of ascertaining whether there is sufficient interest taken in the subject to encourage the commencement of so large and costly an undertaking.

J. O. HALLIWELL-PHILLIPPS.

Hollingbury Copse,
Brighton,
3rd April, 1880.

NOTE.

The foregoing letter appeared in *The Athenæum* of April the 10th, and the correspondence it has elicited has been wholly of a gratifying and encouraging character. I find, however, on careful enquiry, that the mode of publication therein suggested is surrounded by insuperable difficulties, that is to say, if I retain, as I desire, a perfect independence of action, with freedom from all subscription and publishing troubles. Instead, therefore, of commencing a series that might seem to demand continuation, I propose to issue a number of small occasional volumes, of various sizes and of limited impression, each one to be a separate work in itself. Thus, there will be one volume on the Davenant scandal, another on the Globe Theatre, a third on the deer-stealing adventure, another on the poet's last illness, and so on. These will be submitted at intervals to public auction in London, so that an intending purchaser can give a commission to his bookseller even for a single volume, which, as has been previously observed, will in each case form a distinct publication in itself.

LETTER FROM COLONEL CHESTER.

London, 11 May, 1880.

DEAR MR. HALLIWELL-PHILLIPPS,

Here is a crucial illustration of the axiom that there was no standard of orthography for surnames down to so late as the latter part of the seventeenth century. I have before me the old parish register of St. Albans Abbey, and it appears that in February, 1680, a Mr. John Wiltshire, according to modern orthography, had three children baptized. The entries were made by the same scribe at the same instant, and yet, in three consecutive lines, he wrote the surname respectively,—

> Wilcksheir.
> Wilcheir.
> · Wiltcher.

I do not think that I have ever come across a more flagrant instance, and so I communicate it to you.

Sincerely yours,

JOS. L. CHESTER.

J. O. HALLIWELL-PHILLIPPS, ESQ.

www.ingramcontent.com/pod-product-compliance
Lightning Source LLC
Chambersburg PA
CBHW031322280626
47169CB00019B/2821